SCIENCE DIS COVERY

PLANTS AND ANIMALS

Alan Ward

Watts Books

London • New York • Sydney

© 1993 Watts Books

Watts Books
96 Leonard Street
London
EC2A 4RH

Franklin Watts, Inc
387 Park Avenue South
New York, NY 10016

Franklin Watts Australia
14 Mars Road
Lane Cove
NSW 2006

UK ISBN: 0 7496 1143 X

10 9 8 7 6 5 4 3 2 1

Printed in Great Britain

A CIP catalogue record for this
book is available from the
British Library

Dewey Decimal
Classification: 574

Editor: Pippa Pollard
Designer: Mike Snell
Artist: Michael Lye

CONTENTS

BE A NATURE DETECTIVE

To a nature detective, a winding silvery trail, like cellophane, is a clue or a sign that a slug or a snail has crawled by recently. The observant nature detective is able to tell a twiggy 'witches' broom' growth (often on a birch tree) from a clump of evergreen mistletoe, or the untidy drey-nest of a grey squirrel from a pile of dead leaves in the fork of a tree. Are you a nature detective?

Look for clues all around you. Notice old birds' nests in leafless trees, such as a magpie's hollow ball of sticks, a wood pigeon's platform of twigs, or the mud-lined grassy cup made by a thrush last spring.

If you hear tapping on a stone you may be near a thrush's anvil. A blacksmith uses a lump of metal called an anvil when hammering soft metal to make horseshoes. A song thrush uses a stone as an anvil when it grips a snail in its beak and hammers the shell against a stone, to break the shell open and release the snail meat. You may find dozens of smashed snail shells around a thrush's anvil.

Damaged hazel nuts show signs of the animals that broke them open. A squirrel uses its teeth to split a shell. The nuthatch wedges the nut in a crack in the bark of a tree, before using its beak to smash it open. A woodpecker makes a special groove to hold a nut while it chisels it open.

A magpie stole this egg from a nest, and ate the rich yolk inside the shell.

A bird of prey, such as a hawk, plucked these feathers from a bird it had killed for food. It flew away with the meaty part, leaving the feathers behind.

A squirrel stripped this pine cone, while searching for oily pine seeds inside the rough scales.

Some insects lay their eggs inside leaves. A worm-like larva hatches from an egg and starts to feed on the green stuff. It makes a winding tunnel, or 'mine', inside the leaf. The tunnel gets wider as the insect grows fatter.

The trail of the leaf-mining moth has a single dark line along the middle.

The trail of the leaf-mining fly is marked by twin black lines.

BIRDS IN YOUR GARDEN

Can you name the birds that visit your garden? Some common garden birds are the blackbird, blue tit, great tit, hedge sparrow, robin, chaffinch, thrush, house sparrow, starling and greenfinch.

Learn to identify the common garden birds. Borrow or buy a bird book that has large, accurate coloured pictures of everyday birds. A pair of binoculars is useful for birdwatching, but not essential. Birds are scared by sudden movements. Try to keep out of sight. Make a 'viewing window' with brown paper that has holes cut in it for you to look through.

Write a list of every kind of bird that visits your garden (or school grounds) each day over a week. If you see a bird on your list on another day, put a tick against its name. Carry out this survey in spring, summer, autumn and winter, and see if your lists change.

Woodpecker

Magpie

Swallow

Blackbird

Thrush

Collard Dove

Starling

Sparrow

Hedge sparrow

Sparrow

Attracting birds to your garden

You can attract birds into your garden by feeding them in winter. (It is better to let them feed themselves and their young ones in summer.) From autumn until spring, put out finely-chopped food scraps, such as bacon rind, cold potato, cake and cheese. Make sure the food doesn't have salt or a sauce on it.

Bird seed and bird nuts can be bought at supermarkets and pet shops. Scatter the seed where birds will be safe from cats — but also within sight of your viewing place.

Blackbirds enjoy sultanas. Other birds may be tempted by a dish of custard! What other favourite foods do birds have?

If small birds are being bullied by larger ones, make a feeder like this from a shelter standing in a bucket of sand, covered with 5 cm-wide wire mesh.

Hang a bag of nuts from an old tray nailed to a tall post. Put food on the tray. Put out a shallow dish of water for bathing and drinking.

Common plants that will draw birds to your garden include holly, hawthorn, bramble, privet and ivy. These supply shelter, nesting sites and food.

GROWING THINGS

Seeds are the beginnings of new plants. A seed has enough food inside it for it to grow into a baby plant or seedling. As soon as a seedling's leaves appear it can start to make its own food and begin to grow into a mature plant.

Usually, seeds grow invisibly in the ground. Here is an experiment you can do to let you see a seed grow into a seedling.

YOU NEED:

- a large jam jar
- blotting paper
- broad bean or pea seeds

Soak the seeds in water for a day. They should absorb water through their skins and swell up. Roll up a piece of blotting paper to fit inside the jar. Fill the jar with water. Pour the excess water away, leaving a little amount in the bottom of the jar.

'Sow' one of the swollen beans by wedging it between the jar and the paper, near the top of the jar. Put the jar in a warm place, such as near a window, but not where the sun will dry everything up.

Did you know?

A young plant in the ground uses its roots to take in water and chemicals from the soil. It also takes in carbon dioxide gas from the air, through its leaves. These substances are made into food inside the plant's leaves. A plant gets the energy for this from the sun.

It is not always necessary to grow plants from seeds.

Trees from twigs

Cut or break off some twigs from a willow tree. Fill the jar with water. Stand the twigs in the water for several weeks. Keep adding fresh water.

Tiny white blisters should appear on the underwater parts of the twig stems. Be patient, and you will see the white blisters develop into a jungle of roots. Do not worry when the old leaves fall off. New leaves will grow from buds.

YOU NEED:

- willow twigs
- a glass jar
- water

Dish garden

You can use the tops of root vegetables to grow an indoor garden.
Put a few root tops in the dish and pack the marbles or stones around them. Add water to the dish so that the stones are just covered. Be patient and your root garden will grow, with clusters of fresh leaves. Keep your garden in a warm, light place, but do not let it dry up.

YOU NEED:

- root vegetable tops (about 4 cm high)
- a baking dish
- marbles or small stones
- water

BUTTERFLY WATCHING

'Brimstone' means 'yellow like sulphur'. The brilliant yellow male brimstone is supposed to be the original butter-coloured fly that gave its name to all butterflies.

A few butterflies hibernate by passing the winter in a deep, sleep-like trance. The first common butterflies to be around in the spring are common hibernators — the small tortoiseshell, the peacock and the comma.

Look and learn

Be able to name the butterflies shown on these pages when you see them in the wild. Other common species you should see include large and small whites, holly blues, ringlets and meadow browns.

Look out for butterflies mating, their bodies joined together. Watch how caterpillars (young butterflies) feed. Watch adult butterflies sucking sugary nectar juice from flowers.

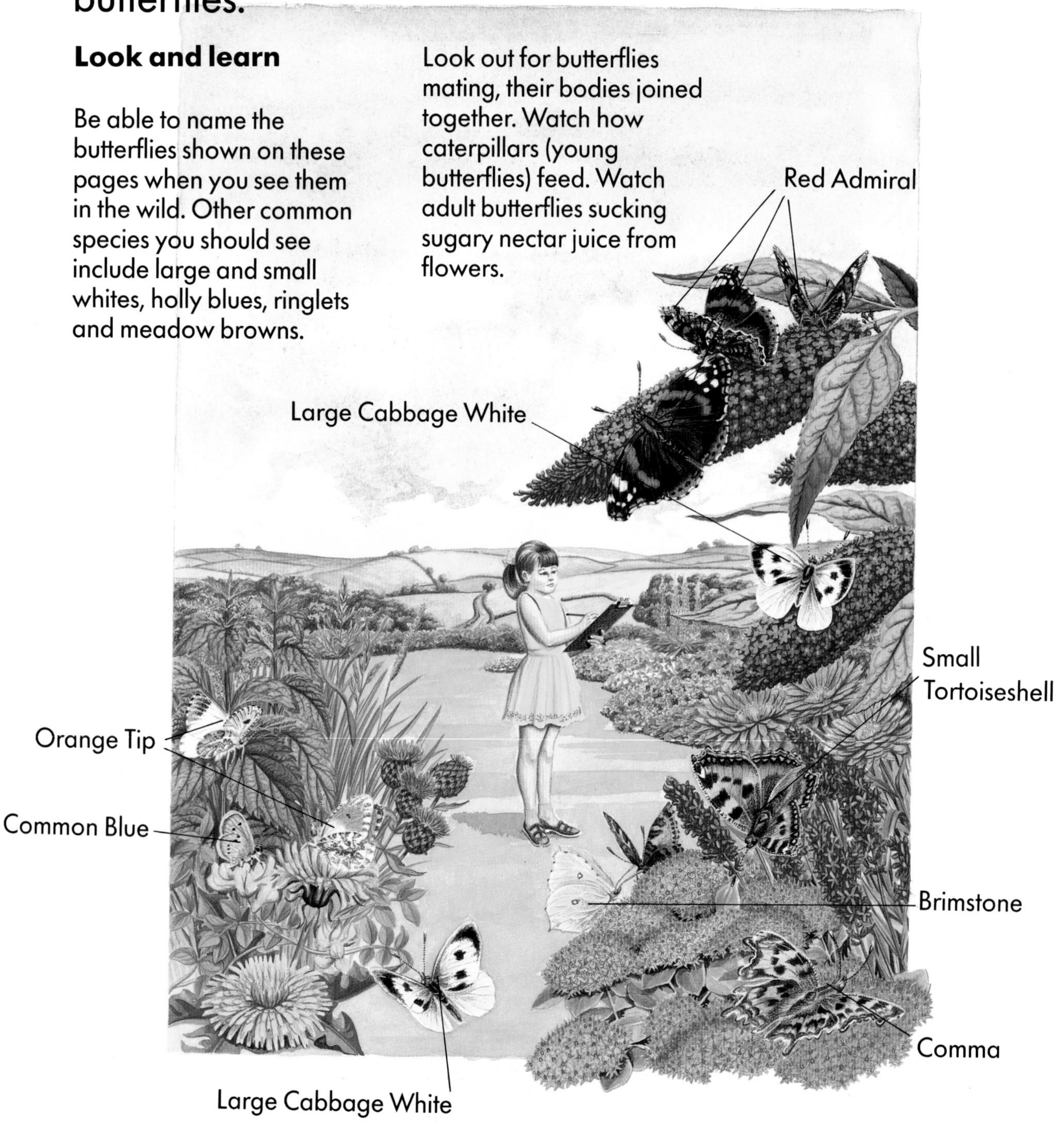

Red Admiral

Large Cabbage White

Small Tortoiseshell

Orange Tip

Common Blue

Brimstone

Large Cabbage White

Comma

Watching caterpillars change into butterflies

Look for caterpillars feeding on stinging nettles. You may find some black peacock butterfly caterpillars. Carefully pick up two or three of them and put them in a plastic bag along with some fresh nettles. Be careful you don't get stung.

Cut a big window in the lid of the box and tape the plastic sheeting over the opening. Stand the box up on its end. Make tiny air holes in the sides of the box. Put the nettles in the jar of water. Pack cotton wool round their stems to prevent the caterpillars from drowning. Gently put the insects on the nettles and close the front of the box with the lid.

Over the next two to three months, watch the life stages of your caterpillars as they feed and grow, change into 'sleeping' chrysalids and finally break out of their chrysalid skins as beautiful butterflies. Let them go in the garden.

YOU NEED:

- a large shoe box with a lid
- a sheet of transparent plastic
- sticky tape
- a jar of water
- cotton wool
- scissors

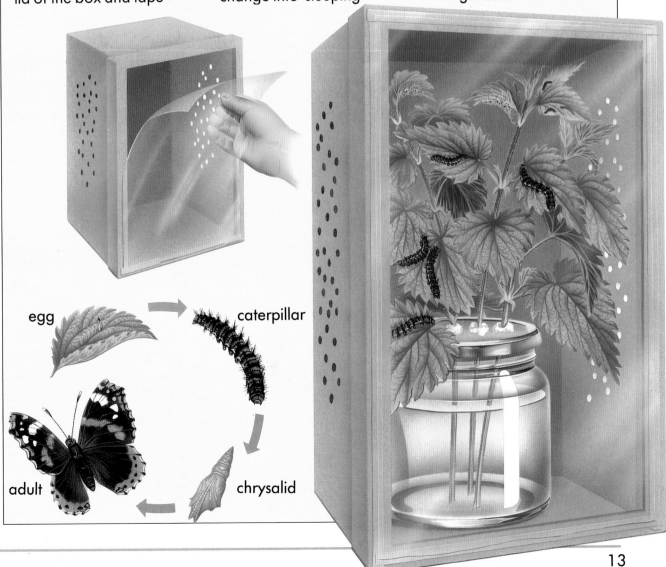

egg

caterpillar

chrysalid

adult

JAM JAR AQUARIUM

A pond is an area of fresh, still water. It is a good example of an ecosystem. It supports a wide variety of plants and animals.

Collecting pond creatures

YOU NEED:

- a long-handled net with a fine mesh
- a bucket
- plastic bags

Ask an adult to accompany you on a trip to a pond. Wear rubber boots and your old clothes. Collect pond water in your bucket. Put mud from the bottom of the pond into a bag. Choose a few pond plants to go in another bag. Then use the net to capture pond animals. Put them into the water in the bucket. About a dozen different creatures will be enough.

When you get home, gently put a pond animal and some pond water in a dish. Study the animal, using a magnifying glass. Can you discover how the creature moves and what it feeds on? Use a reference book on pond life to find out the name of the creature. Examine the other animals you have brought home in this way.

Setting up your jam jar aquarium

Put pond water in the glass jars. Add some pond mud. Let the waters clear. Do not use chlorinated tap water. Tie small stones on to pieces of pond weed and sink them in the separate jars. Put one or two of your animals into each jar. Keep the jars away from the sun, at eye level.

Study your aquarium and make notes about what you see.

YOU NEED:

- white dish or dishes
- large glass jars
- plants and animals collected from a pond

Draw pictures showing details of each animal, such as how many legs, body parts and feelers it has. Put your animals and plants back in the pond when you have finished.

LOVING WEEDS

'A weed is just a flower growing in the wrong place.' Many so-called weeds are beautiful. Daisies light up a lawn in spring. Buttercups glow in the sunlight. Clusters of speedwell form a dreamy mist of blue. How many weeds, or wild flowers, grow in your garden? The pictures on these pages will help you identify some of them. Make a collection of wild flowers from your garden by pressing them.

Pick some wild flowers from your garden. Put them on a sheet of newspaper with another sheet on top. Press them for a few days under the heavy book. When the flowers are dry, tape or glue them on to the plain paper and write their names beside them. Decorate your room with your pressed flower pictures.

YOU NEED:

- newspaper
- plain paper (A4 size)
- sticky tape or glue
- scissors
- a ruler and pen

Put some herb-Robert into a jar of water. Leave the jar on a windowsill with the flowers facing indoors. Watch and wait. Very slowly, the flowers turn to face the sunlight.

What has happened?

Sunlight causes the flower stems to twist towards the sun. This is an example of a plant growth movement, or a tropism.

You may find some ivy-leaved toadflax growing on your garden wall. When its flowers go to seed the stems grow back towards the wall, where the seeds can fall into cracks and grow into new toadflax flowers.

PROJECTS WITH DANDELIONS

Dandelions are like big yellow medals, bright as little suns. They cheer up motorway verges in April and May, when they look their best, but they can be seen in most months of the year.

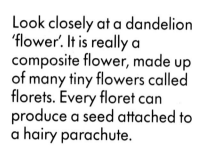

Dandelion seedlings

Line the bottom of the plastic box with lint. Sprinkle water on it to make it damp, but not sopping wet. Space out the seeds (complete with parachutes) on the damp lint. Close the box and put it on a windowsill, but not in direct sunlight.

YOU NEED:

- dandelion seeds
- a transparent plastic box with a lid
- lint (or paper towels)
- water

Watch day by day, to see the seeds detach themselves from their parachutes and start to develop into seedlings.

Look closely at a dandelion 'flower'. It is really a composite flower, made up of many tiny flowers called florets. Every floret can produce a seed attached to a hairy parachute.

Dandelion darts

Pick a single, straight, hollow dandelion stem. It must be clean, empty and dry. This is your blowpipe. Use a dandelion seed as a dart. Insert the seed into one end of the stem. Then blow it out and watch it float away.

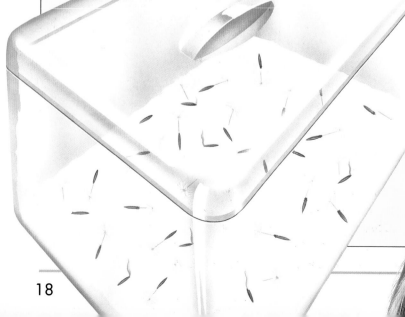

YOU NEED:

- fresh dandelions

Dandelion rubber

The milky-white sap that oozes from the stems and roots of dandelions is a form of latex, a substance from which rubber can be made.

Pick some fresh dandelions. Coat the end of your finger (but not your fingertip) with sap. Let the sap dry. Then roll it off your finger very gently to make a rubber band.

During the Second World War, a variety of dandelion was grown on farms in Russia to provide latex to make rubber tyres for cars and lorries.

Did you know?

People make wine from dandelion flowers and coffee can be made from dandelion roots. The Japanese use sliced dandelion roots as a vegetable. Dandelion leaves can be eaten in a salad. Why not try making a dandelion salad yourself? Ask an adult to help you. Remember to wash the leaves throughly.

Challenge

Try preserving dandelion seed 'clocks', using hair spray.

Dandelion magic

'Dandelion' means 'tooth of a lion'. Look at the leaves of a dandelion and you will see why. Another name for it is 'schoolboy's clock'. The number of breaths needed to blow away the seeds is said to give the time of day to the nearest hour. Yet another name is 'wishes'. If you blow away all the seeds in an odd number of puffs, your wish is supposed to come true.

IS YOUR HOME AN INDOOR SAFARI PARK?

Even if you do not keep pets, there are sure to be wild animals living and sheltering in, or just visiting, your home.

Lacewing fly
This beautiful green insect, with lacey wings and golden eyes, comes indoors for the winter. In spring and summer its young will eat huge numbers of harmful aphids.

Go on safari in your own home

Look for these specimens:

Hibernating small tortoiseshell
The butterfly is sheltering in a dark, quiet place. It wakes up in the spring and starts to flutter about. Set it free before it hurts itself.

Hibernating queen wasp
The wasp may be clinging by her jaws to the inside of the fold of a curtain. She cannot sting you. In the spring she will fly out of the window to find a place to build her nest.

Zebra spider
Watch a little zebra spider prowling after its prey on a sunny windowsill (usually outside). It does not spin a web to catch its food, but pounces on small insects as a cat jumps on a mouse.

YOU NEED:

- a jar (for holding creatures to study)
- a magnifying glass
- a notebook
- a pencil

Beetle

One night in early summer, this large, noisy beetle may blunder into an open window. It is harmless.

Earwig

The earwig probably fell out of a flower. The pincers of the male are curved and the female's are straight. Earwig mothers take care of their little ones. Earwigs eat large numbers of greenfly and other aphid pests.

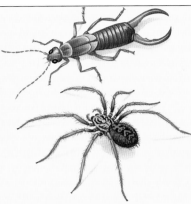

House spider

The house spider is definitely a resident in your home. One may have fallen into the bath, or entered it through a pipe. House spiders spin untidy webs.

Cranefly

The cranefly comes indoors in late summer. Look for its knobbly 'balancers' behind its wings. These vibrate and help the insect keep its balance while flying.

Make a list of the animals you discover in your house. If you find an abandoned paper wasps' nest in the roof, ask an adult to remove it for you so that you can study its delicate walls and cells.

FUN WITH TREES

After measuring thousands of trees, Alan Mitchell, a tree scientist, found a rough way to estimate a tree's age, without having to cut it down and count its annual growth rings.

Estimating the age of a living tree

Mark a spot on the tree trunk 1.5 metres above the ground. Measure the circumference of the trunk at that spot. If the tree is growing out in the open, its approximate age is one year for every 2.5 centimetres of the circumference.

For example:

$$\frac{\text{circumference (cm)}}{2.5}$$

$$\frac{50 \text{ cm}}{2.5} = 20 \text{ years}$$

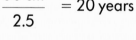

Trees growing in a wood, where there is competition for light, would be twice as old (2 years for every 2.5 cm of the circumference) and trees growing in a line would be half as old again (1 ½ years for every 2.5 cm).

Grow mistletoe

Mistletoe is a parasite – it feeds on another living thing, such as an apple tree. Birds eat mistletoe berries. The sticky seeds from inside the berries often get stuck on the birds' beaks. When they wipe off the seeds on trees, the seeds take root in the bark. Early March is a good time to force a mistletoe berry into a crack in the bark of an apple tree. You can cover the seed with fine wire netting to stop birds from pecking it out. Mistletoe plants take a few years to grow into big clumps, so be patient.

Did you know?

A quick way to estimate the height of a tree is to get a friend to stand against it. You also need a long ruler and a tape measure. Ask an adult to help you. Stand well back and use the ruler to work out how many times the height of your friend is the height of the tree. Then measure your friend's true height with the tape measure. Multiply it by how many times taller the tree is proportionally to find out the tree's real height.

Leaf skeletons

YOU NEED:

- hard, shiny tree leaves, such as ivy, laurel, horse-chestnut, holly and aspen
- a bucket of rainwater
- fresh water
- a small knife (be careful)

Soak the leaves in the rainwater for several weeks outside. They will get smelly, but do not change the water. When the leaves have rotted, use the knife to carefully peel away their top and bottom skins.

You are left with 'skeletons' of the leaf veins. Pick them clean and wash them in fresh water. Mount the dried skeletons on cards, or use them in decorations.

ANIMAL MAGIC

YOU NEED:

- a wooden board (roughly 50 cm square)
- a plate
- a big round bowl
- chalk
- garden snails

Summer is the best time to do this, but choose a cool place. First find some garden snails and shrubbery. They should all be about the same size. Then get together with some friends for a day at the Snail Races!

Use the wooden board to make your racing track. Draw around the plate with the chalk to make a circular starting place in the middle. Then draw around the bowl, to make a circular finishing line. The inner and outer circles must be the same distance apart all the way round.

Carefully put the snails inside the inner circle. The winning snail is the first one to cross the line of the outer circle.
Let your snails go again when you have finished with them.

Did you know?
A champion garden snail could probably manage to do a five-and-a-half day mile. Can you find a supersnail?

Did you know?
Ladybirds like to nibble a moist lump of sugar.

How fast is a garden snail?

Put your snail down on a flat, damp, paved surface. Follow it moving for five minutes. Mark its trail with the chalk. Then place the string along the chalked line. Cut it to the length of the trail and measure it.

If a snail goes 40 cm in 5 minutes (a twelfth of an hour), it might go 40×12 cm in a full hour. That is a speed of 480 cm, or 4.8 metres per hour.

Ladybird wings

Do you remember the balancers behind the cranefly's wings on page 19? They were once a second pair of wings. A ladybird's shiny, bright red shell-like wing covers were also wings once. The wings a ladybird uses to fly with now are neatly folded under the wing covers.

If you can catch a ladybird in your hand, let it crawl up one of your fingers. When it gets to the top, it raises its wing covers, unfolds its delicate wings and flies away. Notice how the wing covers are held open during flight.

When a ladybird falls on its back it uses its wing covers as levers to force itself upright. Gently put your ladybird on its back. Watch how it rights itself again. When ladybirds are frightened they may flip over on to their backs deliberately, tucking in their legs and pretending to be dead.

Let your ladybird go when you have finished. Put it on a plant infested by aphids. You may see it munch up an aphid snack.

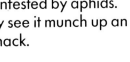

PLANT MAGIC

A-maze-ing potato

Cut away half of one of the short sides of the box. Glue the cards inside the box, like screens. Put the potato plant in the box in the corner diagonally opposite the hole cut in one side. Close the lid. The potato shoot should, in time, wend its way out of the simple maze.

Can a plant get out of a more complicated maze?

What has happened?
The sensitive growing tip of the shoot is attracted by the light. Light provides essential energy, without which the plant would die.

Did you know?
When rhubarb leaves are soaked in a bucket of water for a few days and the water then splashed around the roots of plants infested with aphids, the pests are said to depart.

26

Cherries that burst

YOU NEED:

- ripe cherries
- a bowl of water

Soak the ripe cherries in the water. Wait for a few hours, looking at the fruit from time to time to see what is happening. The cherries should swell and eventually burst. In very wet weather, cherries sometimes split while they are still on the tree.

What has happened?

There are tiny pores in a cherry's skin. These little holes are so small that you need a microscope to see them. Water can easily get in through these holes, but the thick, sugary juice in the cherry cannot escape.

The extra water that the cherries absorbed increased the amount of juice inside them and put pressure on their skins until they burst. The process by which the water was absorbed through the pores in the cherry skins is called osmosis.

Greenhouse effect

You may have seen a bottle with a fruit, such as a pear, inside it, and wondered how this trick was done.

Select a healthily growing pear, small enough to go inside the bottle neck. Do not pick it, but trim away some of the leaves on its stem. Poke the pear on its stem inside the bottle. Then support the bottle by tying it to a sturdy twig on the same tree. The bottle should be exposed to sunlight.

By autumn the pear will have grown inside the bottle and will be far too fat to be taken out. Cut free the pear and stop it going bad by filling the bottle with vinegar.

YOU NEED:

- a fruiting pear tree early in summer
- scissors and string
- a wine or milk bottle

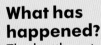

What has happened?

The bottle acted as a small greenhouse. Heat rays from the sun warmed the air inside the bottle to make the pear grow. It was not so easy for heat to escape from the bottle.

NATURE TRAIL

Many ordinary gardens have enough different animals and plants in them for you to convert them into interesting nature trails. Ask an adult for permission before you do this.

YOU NEED:

- sticks
- drawing pins
- cardboard
- scissors
- pens and coloured paints
- a ruler

Explore your garden to find some plants and small animals. Use a nature book to identify them if you don't know what they are.

Choose around nine places of interest in your garden. Mark a winding trail, using cardboard arrows on sticks, to connect the places of interest. Write a sign for each place, explaining what there is to see. Fix the signs on to sticks and put them around your nature trail.

Invite your neighbours and friends to visit your nature trail.

Here is a nature trail around a garden:

① Search the berberis for bees on the small flowers.

② Look up at the house to see wasps going to and from their nest. The paper nest is under a roof tile. The wasps may be carrying pats of chewed wood 'paper', or parts of insects to feed their young.

③ Can you identify these wild flowers?

④ Lift up stones to see woodlice. They prefer the damp and darkness — and are related to lobsters that live in the sea.

⑤ Notice the thin insects standing on the water of the pond, without getting their feet wet! They are pond-skaters. They use their beak-like mouths to stab smaller insects, before sucking out their body juices.

⑥ A fox may visit the garden at night in search of earthworms, one of its main foods. Look for its footprints in the morning.

⑦ Notice the cherry stones left with holes gnawed by wood mice. Can you see the teeth marks?

⑧ Wasps, bees and butterflies feed off green ivy flowers in autumn. Wood pigeons take the dark green berries in winter.

GLOSSARY

A

aphid
A small insect that sucks plant juices, such as a greenfly.

absorb
To soak up.

B

balancers
Tiny structures that grow instead of back wings on a fly. When the insect is flying, they vibrate up and down and help the fly to keep its balance.

bud scale
A plate-like leaf that protects a plant bud.

C

caterpillar
The larva in the life cycle of butterflies or moths.

chrysalid
The form that certain insects take in the resting stage of their life cycle. Inside the skin of a chrysalid the form of the larva is changed into the form of the adult insect.

circumference
The distance around the edge of a circle.

composite
Made up of several parts.

E

ecosystem
The balance of animals and plants in a particular environment.

environment
The space in which an animal or plant lives.

G

greenhouse effect
Acting like a greenhouse by holding in the heat.

H

hibernate
To pass the winter in a deep state of rest.

L

larva
The body form of certain insects in which most of the growth in size takes place.

latex
A milky juice from certain plants, such as rubber trees.

N

nature trail
A specially-built pathway from which nature can be observed and studied.

nymph
The form of the young animal in the life cycle of certain insects, such as grasshoppers and earwigs, that do not have larval forms.

P

parasite
A living thing that feeds on the body of another living thing.

preserve
To keep from harm or to prevent from rotting away.

R

root hair
A special hair on the root of a plant, through which water and other chemicals can pass into the plant.

S

seedling
A young plant that has grown from seed.

T

tropism
The growth of a plant towards a particular influence, such as light or gravity.

Y

yolk
The yellow part of an egg.

INDEX